DOLPHINS

DOLPHINS

Stephen Spender

St. Martin's Press
New York

ISBN 0-312-11264-5
ISBN 0-312-11288-2 (limited edition)

First published in Great Britain by Faber and Faber Limited.

First U.S. Edition: September 1994
10 9 8 7 6 5 4 3 2 1

Some of these poems
appeared first in
Horizon, the *Times Literary Supplement*,
Stand and the *London Magazine*.

Contents

DOLPHINS

Dolphins

Happy, they leap
Out of the surface
Of waves reflecting
The sun fragmented
To broken glass
By the stiff breeze
Across our bows.

Curving, they draw
Curlicues
And serifs with
Lashed tail and fin
Across the screen
Of blue horizon –
Images
Of their delight
Outside, displaying
My heart within.

Across this dazzling
Mediterranean
August morning
The dolphins write such
Ideograms:
With power to wake
Me prisoned in
My human speech
They sign:
'I AM!'

Her House

The city left behind them, they drove on
Past factories, suburbs, farms.
                                        She saw
Suddenly, from a hill, the coast
Outlined by surf, and rocks that seemed
The shadows of the surf.
                                        'My house!' she cried,
Pointing in triumph where it stood
High on a cliff above a bay.

The slate roof gleamed like dove feathers
And in the fanned façade tall windows
Mirrored on glass panes the garden
Between whose dazzling colours loomed
The shadowy interior
Cut through with glints of gold.

'My house!
My house for which I've scraped and saved
These thirty years! My house I've driven
All day to boast to you, dear friend!'

        Leaving the main road then, she drove
Down a steep lane between tall hedges
Whose branches, high up, interlocked.
'This tunnel of dense leaves,' she thought,
'Is minutes of eternity
Through which I have to press to reach my house.'

But when at last she reached the light,
All she was sure was hers had vanished
– No house, no friend, no car.
                              She was
Alone, dressed in a shroud, beholding
The quivering fury of the desert
Where crackling thorn and cactus blazed.

                    *

          High on a sandstone cliff, there stood
Figures in shrouds hewn out of sandstone
Who raised grave hands in salutation
To her who, kneeling to them, prayed:
'Have you no nook or cranny to let me in?'

And woke elate in certainty
She shared the eternal desert, theirs.

Lines for Roy Fuller

Lines of yours I first read were of war
In Africa: your being *moved across*
Two oceans and *bored systematically*
By army life: and your eyes opened onto
Ultimate truth: which is – *the terrible*.

Reading your words then, I saw soldiers
Silhouetted against bare sky
With their machines: those instruments
For killing, being killed: tank, gun,
In the arena of the scorpion.

One flesh-like thing was that mauve flower
Which, between thorns, the cactus shows:
Defenceless as those young men's faces
Naked above their battle dress –
Their camouflage of scrub and sand.

Carpaccio painted such a scene:
Soldiers – helmets – breast-plates – skulls –
Cactus – a dragon. Standing there,
A hermit with eyes deep as wells
Piercing the desert, like your lines.

Air Raid

In this room like a bowl of flowers filled with light
Family eyes look down on the white
Pages of a book, and the white ceiling
Like starch of a nurse, reflects a calm feeling.

The daughter, with hands outstretched to the fire,
Transmits through her veins the peaceful desire
Of the family tree, from which she was born,
To push tendrils through dark to a happier dawn.

In the ancient house or the glass-and-steel flat
The vertical descendants of the genes that
Go back far in the past, are supported by floors
And protected by walls from the weather outdoors.

In their complex stage settings they act out the parts
Of their bodies enclosing their human hearts
With limbs utilizing chairs, tables, cups,
All the necessities and props.

They wear the right clothes and go the right ways,
Read the news, and play golf, and fill out their days
With hobbies, meals brought from the kitchen range.
And no one sees anything eerie or strange

In all this. And perhaps they are right. Nothing is
Until an unreasoning fury impinges
From an enemy's vision of life, on their hearth.
And explodes. And tears their loved home down to earth.

Then the inside-turned-outside faces the street.
Rubble decently buries the dead human meat.
Piled above it, a bath, wardrobe, books, telephone
Though all who could answer its ringing have gone.

Standing unscathed is one solitary wall,
Half a floor attached, forgotten to fall.
Convolvulus patterns of pink and blue line
That rectangle high up where they once used to dine.

Bemused passers-by are bound to observe
That inside-shown-outside like the deep curve
Of mother-o'-pearl exposed in a shell
Where a mollusc, long smashed, at one time did dwell.

But the house has been cracked in an enemy's claws,
Years of love ground down to rubble in jaws,
And the tender sensitive life thrown away
By the high-flying will of the enemy's day.

(*Horizon*, February 1941. 1993)

Letter from an Ornithologist in Antarctica

(Remembering S.B.O.)

Happy, you write, I am, happy to go alone
On the cable chair from Palmer Station (where our base is)
Across 'Hero Inlet' to 'Bonaparte Point'
(Just a bare rock attached to a crumbling glacier!)
Where at night I fumble stones for baby petrels
Until the cold has made my fingers freeze –
And I cannot tell the chicks apart from stones
Nor feel the cable well for my return.

Most nights are cloudy, always overcast,
But sometimes I peek stars through cloud-rifts –
Once Halley's Comet in a cloud ripped open.

One night the sky was clear, no wind, air balmy,
And I lay snug in gloves and sweater
Happy to be alone but also happy
To think of my companions near by
Connected to me by that cable –
And that six hundred miles far north the tip
Of Tierra del Fuego has some settlers
(Four hundred further north there come real towns).

Then, as I watched the sky, I saw six stars
Move, and I speculated that space satellites
– Those man-made messengers on starry errands

Of espionage, war, TV – good or evil –
Converge over the Pole. Happy I felt then
Out there, in space, those distances made human.

Farewell to My Student

For our farewell, we went down to the footpath
Circling the lake.
                    You stood there, looking up at
Egrets nesting in high branches

– White ghosts in a green tapestry.

And I stood silent, thinking of
Images to recall this moment.

The first must surely be that pine tree
Bark slashed with gold, leaning across
The blue lines of the lake beyond.

Then, stamped upon the day, your face.

                    Perhaps Bellini
Delved from antiquity such an image
Of a twenty-year-old Triton, against waves
Blowing on a conch;

And Seurat, centuries later, in the profile
Of a hallooing boy against the Seine.

But then you turned to me and said
With that mild glance, a third thing to remember:

'You are gone already, your thoughts far from here
At least three thousand miles away
Where you will be tomorrow.'

Then ten years passed till, today, I write these lines.

Laughter

That time you laughed
Fell over on the floor laughing

And then my laughter too caught fire
One blaze of both our laughing

Remembered across distances long after

Not gone not gone not altogether
Extinguished by the Ice Age of your death.

When you were living
It lingered in the world
Among things only put aside
In cupboards – letters, clothes,
Photographs taken on that journey
We went together

All now become
On one side – yours – pure absence
On mine, that vacuum
Nature, we are told, abhors:

Which now the memory of our laughing
Rushes in to fill.

History and Reality

I

Escaped from Germany –
Cared for by English friends, with whom
Kindness counted still –

Rumours reached her –

Photographs made by the Gestapo –

Jews, her people –
So various, all one –

Each taken full-face –

The strong – the meek – the sad – the proud.

*

Hunger had stretched the parchment skin
Across the contours of the bone –
Forehead, cheek-bones, chin.

And in each face there was the same
Ultimate revelation
Of eyes that stared upon the real –

Some terrible final thing.

She locked herself inside her room,
Her mind filled with those images
From Germany, her homeland, where
Those deaths were the reality –

Real! – not some tragedy that actors
Performed before an audience –
Pity and terror purifying
The onlooker, enraptured by
Poetry secreted in the lines.
But where the players were the victims
Massacred from a tyrant's mouth.

※

She felt a kind of envy for
Those who stood naked in their truth:
Where to be of her people was
To be one of those millions killed.

She starved her body to pure thought
To be one with her people snatched
From ghettos by the SS, then
Hurled into cattle trucks of trains
Hurtling all night across bare plains
Till dawn, when there stood, waiting on
Platforms of sidings (below walls
Of concrete and barbed wire) – guards, who
Marched them to a parade-ground, where
Those fit to work in factories
Were separated from the rest –
Women and children, the old, the sick,

Who, taken to a yard, were robbed
Of jewellery, satchels, playthings, shoes –
Things that to them meant home and name –
And made to stand there when a voice
From a watch-tower proclaimed they would
Be cleansed of lice, and being Jews.

IV

Then thrust inside a shed where she
Through her intense imagining
Stood there among them bodily
When, from outside, the guards turned on
Taps through which hissed not water but
The murdering gas, whereon that crowd
Breathed a great sigh of revelation –
Their life, their death – for her the real
Instant where history ground its wheel
On her with them, inside that moment
When – outside – truth was only words.

The Half of Life

(To Barry Humphries)

Half his life gone, he takes his drink
In the café in the park. Across
Oblongs of marble table-tops
Lights and shadows travel, arrowing from
The sun, through wind-stirred leaves above.

Lifting his spoon, he lets it ring
Idly against his glass, and thinks
'The time that took to sound sums up
All my life lived till now, contained
Within the instant it was struck.

'But when I leave here, setting out
On that half life that's still to come,
Each lived-through moment will weigh on
My pulses – work, war, boredom, love
Experienced each as a whole world.

'Then, at the end, when I return
To sit down here at my old place
Amongst those young as I am now
(I'll think "They're young as I was then")
All my past life will seem one shadow
Cast by the sun on a white stone.'

The Palatine Anthology

(To Charles Causley)

Above, there is a firmament of stars
Two thousand light-years distant from us.

Some names still pierce us with their light
Anacreon, Callimachus –

Plato still scrawls across those skies:
'Would that I had your million eyes
To gaze down on my friend – star-gazing
From Earth. His eyes would have no choice
Then, but meet mine.'

One poet is *Anonymous*:

Out of his whole life he chose
This instant of intensest flame!
Having attained which climax, he
Let fall a canister through space –

His burned-out no-name.

Have-Beens

        have sometimes the feeling
That they're not here at all, not of this day
Ordered by the clock-hand in every particular
All over the world, the ticking minute,
But of another place that has no time-table
Except in having been all equally buried
Under the lid, the crust of the present,
In Hades where all pasts are contemporaneous
Simply in having been: the swords shields helmets
Of the *Iliad*'s prehistory, in the same junkyard
As the shells and dug-outs of the Western Front.

Poètes Maudits

Under the X-ray sun, two *poètes*
Maudits sit drinking absinthe: *Paul,*
Lecherously lachrymose at having
Abandoned wife, child, priest, for *Rimb,*
Heaven-born boy with Hellfire tongue,
Hair a torn halo round his head
And eyes that gaze deep in his glass.

Drunken on language, they hurl down,
In rivalry between them, boasts –
Each clamouring he had the more
Obscene childhood, spent all day
Crouching in holes of latrines, spying
Up at those parts the grown-ups hide
Under pious hypocrisies
Of hymns sung, sermons preached, in church:
Cocks cunts arse-holes from out of whose
Passages issue piss shit blood,
Excremental extremities
Dictionaries grudge four letters to
And doctors bury in deep tomes
Of dead words in dead languages
Like Latin names inscribed on tombs.

Delirious with ecstasy
Of shames let fly against the sun
Rimb leaps up on the table, tears

18

His clothes apart above the knees
And shows embossed upon one thigh
A cicatrice like a medallion.
'My gilded stamp of sin,' he cries,
'That I was born with, my true self.'

Ecstatic at such innocence
Of shames let fly against the sun
Paul, slobbering, rises from his chair
And plants his tongue upon that place.

White with contempt, the boy taunts him:
'Mad aunt! Crazed shepherdess! Fuck off!'
And knocks *Paul* down. *Paul* rises, feels
Inside the darkness of a pocket
A gun that yearns to reach its target,
Rimb's ice-black heart, the centre of
Their love turned hate: and aiming at
That centre, misses, wounds a finger.

The boy, become all child again,
Runs to his mother's womb – 'Police! Help!
Maman!' Two gendarmes rushing in
Take *Paul* away, to spend two years
Spieling poems – his penances!

II PARIS 1873

Rimb rushes from the café, walks
With scything strides past fields hills towns
All day, and all night, sleepless, sees
Written across the dark his one
True poem true world of childhood, when,
At cock-crow, from his mother's house

He saw rainbows of dew cling on
Threads spiders wove between grass blades
Of meadows where hares raced with thudding
Reverberant hind legs that struck
The dawn's delirium like a drum,
While from low cottages small children
Ran out and pranced in jeering rings
Round steeples of their praying mothers.

*

Strode on and on till he reached Paris
That earliest hour when light and dark
Are ghosts laid in each other's arms,
Merged within one grey monochrome,
And the grey houses their own tombs –

When street cleaners come out to hose
Down avenues –
And in shirt sleeves
Waiters to tables set on pavements –
To throw out drunks in whose gross heads
Last night's brawls still reverberate –

When clattering shutters of shop windows
Rise upon bank clerks walking in
Circles of clocks that toll their lives –

III COMMUNE 1870

Beyond these *Rimb* saw his own ghost
Of two years past, the runaway –
1870, year of
Germany invading France –

Spike-helmeted jack-booted Prussians
Goose-stepping through French villages –

Yet at the centre Paris stood –
The flaming torch of all the free –
The Revolutionary Commune –

The People's Cause that called to him
Which, answering, he smuggled
IIs body through the Prussian lines

To Paris where, at a caserne
Of Communards, he brought that prize –
Freedom! his life to fight for theirs –
Freedom! – the workers' soldiers' sailors'
Deserters' pimps' whores' – such canaille
Shooting at sewage rats for food –

He brought them his rebellious youth
Which they received with jeers and blows
Obscenities and rape that pierced
His desecrated heart they spat
Out of their mouths with wads of chewed
Tobacco quids back to the gutter –

Back to his village and his mother.

IV VISIONARY

There, where he hid inside a barn
And cast his childhood from him, and
Cut himself off from all he knew,
His world from being human, 'Us',
But willed his 'I' be object 'IT'

On which the external history struck
Sounding below 'I' to ANOTHER
Deeper than conscious self which was
Visionary, Prophet, Magus of
One unreal final ultimate
Of Hell or Heaven, a new Love where
Poem knew poem as truth, as now
His poems knew *Paul*'s, as *Paul*'s knew his,
Poems that made love to poets, their makers.

V PARIS 1872

Paul to join whom he fled to Paris
Paul who received him as a god

And showed him off to drunk Parnassians
Took him to salons of Princesses –
Boy genius – wonder of a season –
Holy and damned – Saint Sebastian
And Satan – out of whose mouth streamed
Beauty and terror – all his world –
Impenetrable blazing diamond.

VI VIE LITTERAIRE

And yet some primal instinct in him
Of pagan slave or Gallic spunk
Detested them – the hostesses –
The inky scribes of feuilletons –

Also the poets – their scented beards –
Their agate eyes – their hearts laid bare –
Their childhoods weeping with dead mothers –
Their Testimonies and senile rhymes –

The paper-thin *vie littéraire*

And most of all he hated *Paul*
His cloying friend with heart that streamed
With blood for him the sneering boy –
And yet denied *Rimb's* jeered demand
That *Paul* leave wife and babe for him.

*

Rimb spat these from his mouth and strode
From Paris – whore of whores – to face
Past its Hell-gates, the modern world . . .

VII VOYAGES 1876–80

London – Milan – Stuttgart – Vienna –
On foot – trains – ships –

From Harderwijk on the Zuyder Zee
– Conscript of the Dutch colonial army –

On the *Prins van Oranje* –

  Skipped ship at Samarang –
Javanese jungles – natives –

Worked his way back

Bremen – Stockholm – Copenhagen –

Foreman of Mazeran-Viannay-Bardey –
Construction workers –
Cypriots – Greeks – Syrians –

*

The sky a lottery from which
He drew his fiery ticket –
Africa! – Hurrah! – Harar!
Director of the Agence Pinchard.

*

(Remains one photograph of *Rimb*
White-suited bristle-haired bronzed –

An explorer's eyes of ice that gaze
Past sacks of coffee-beans and heaps
Of animal-skins – and bottles –
Account books – ledgers –

Dreaming of mapping Zanzibar.)

VIII THE COMMUNIST MANIFESTO

O Capitalism
Imagination of the Real –
Captains of Industry,
Explorers, engineers, inventors –
Entrepreneurs,
Hearts of stone and brains of steel

History material on which
You chisel artefacts
– Canals
Incised through isthmuses –
Where two converging oceans kiss –

– And laying railways down
Across the continents – like arms
Of populations separated

Millennially till then
Embracing between mountain chains
On plains and valleys, their love beds.

*

Also the gold stored in the banks.

IX CAPITALIST 1880–90

Rimb   capitalist —
Grown to full height with power to shape
The external world to match his will –

(Rejecting poetry's mirages)

Yet behind all
It is the dream that drives him on –
The dream that vows
It will come true.

*

That after many journeyings
Of his crammed caravanserai
From weather-dented coasts – inland
Through deserts scattered with great stones
Locking within them memories
Of cities once raised on their columns –

To the interior of
The heart-shaped continent –

And after trading there with natives –
(Their scriptural black faces masks
Through which their bargaining eyes watched his) –

Bartering his medicine – beads – TRASH! –
With them for spices – ivory – gold –

After unending boredom of
Delays delays delays caused by
Bad faith – debts – credit to be raised
(Credit from Paris – hard to raise!) –

After infernal nights in rooms
Where stings of insects left in him
Fevers endemic to that zone –
His hard lithe body furrowed with
Trenches of premature old age –

After all these, he would return
Home to his village and his mother
And, standing on the threshold there,
Aged, lean, penitent, he'd watch
Where she sat stooped among her ruins –
Her stiff, starched pieties his fury
Was chariot over, linked with *Paul*'s:
Their ecstasy's excesses of
Red dreams released to violence by
Hashish and absinthe: journeys to
Cities the brothels of their wills.

*

But, to her, Africa was manifest
Insanity, his poems come true:
Continent of barbarian
Ebony natives, wielding spears,
Warring with naked tribes, their foes;
And, in the desert, gold-maned lions

26

Pouncing upon their prey – her son;
And in the jungle, serpents coiled,
Dropping from branches, on her son.

*

Then, entering her room, he would say:
'Mother, I am your son, returned –
No more the poet who made of words
Artefacts nothing but his dreams,
Shadows in light, mere fantasies –
Unreal vacuity.
                    Now I come,
Real magic valid in my hands,
Real wand of gold I gained, to change
Your poverty to riches, make
The palace dreamed come true. I am
The poem made solid that is real.'

x HOME 1886–91

3500 francs in gold
Gunrunning from the coast –

Then suddenly there died
Proposed companions on that journey
Soleillet, Labatut.

And, against all warnings,
He went alone,
Travelling four months with
34 cameleers, threatening to strike,
30 camels, 2,000 rifles, 75,000 cartridges –

To the camp of Makonnen
Who called the guns 'out-dated'.

Then back to Harar
Where, from the mail awaiting him,
– Catalogues – treatises – bills –
A pamphlet falls – from Paris
A new review – *The Decadent* –
Fit organ of young poets –
An article by *Paul*, discovering
One genius, greatest poet of all,
Rimb –

    who lets the pamphlet fall:

'DISGUSTING   PUERILE   OBSCENE!'

*

Writes home: 'Dear friends,
The cicatrice upon my thigh
Has made the whole limb gangrenous
And thick as all the body.
Having cashed all my savings
And had a litter made
(My own specifications!)
I have hired twenty bearers to
Carry me to the coast.'

*

The sun a red-hot piston rod
From the sky-centre
Pounding down on him – body and soul!
Days of fire and nights of ice
Circles of Hell
Moved through, that are God's Love,

Defied by him as he repeats
Childhood obscenities:
Cock cunt arse-hole etcetera
Spat back at Him.

*

Then at Marseilles, the hospital,
The death they all found beautiful –
Doctor – priest – mother – sister – all . . .

*   *   *

But, as he lay there, dying –
Remembering that cicatrice
Upon his thigh – ('*my gilded
Stamp of sin*,' to *Paul*)
Did he – too ill to speak – ask then:
'Unto what God, of Heaven or Hell
– Spiritual or material –
Poetry or the Real –
Is this, my severed thigh,
Blood-sacrifice?'

Room

This room's electric with those memories
Which, when he enters their invisible
Unanticipated zone, galvanize
His spirit to a shape his body had
Centuries, it seems, ago.
                              Open the door –
The room's ablaze with children
In their sloop made of two chairs
Where they play pirates.
                              Points of fire, their hair,
Their eyes of ice, their laughter
The clashing swords of angels guarding Eden.
'Come in!' they shout, and mean to say 'Get out!'

Then, standing at the window, seeing
Dusk absorb the green particulars
Of grass and trees, and make intenser
The glow of bricks and roses, he hears
Calling from the shrubbery, the voice
Of one long dead,
Poignant through the dark, that when she lived
He dared not answer.

Grandparents

Incredible to realize they've gone:
Matthew – Maro – their children – our grandchildren –
Saskia – Cosima – in the Renault
Festooned as for a wedding, with pink hands
Waving from windows blown farewells.
Matthew's parting smile above the wheel
Disappears down our lane   his face
Torn from a coloured postcard of our garden.
We go back to the house where Yesterday
Still scatters through the rooms the wreckage
Of cardboard boxes, toys, torn silver paper.
Our room that seemed to bulge with voices
And walls bounced off by Matthew's clarinet's
Billowing notes – relapsed to silence. We ourselves
Though ancient, not yet ghosts, feel two-dimensional
– Cardboard cut-outs of grandparents
With one soul, like some flower plucked at a picnic
A century ago – pressed between pages
Of an ancient tome – absorbing ink each side –
One chapter's ending and the next's beginning.

Black-and-White Photography

I

Brilliant lens, miraculous shutter – forceps –
Take up the object and translate it
Simplified to light and shadow –
The silent dead, the insolently living,
The kissed and kissing loved –
Translated now into the two-dimensional
Bright flowers of yesterday recorded, albumed in
The traveller's returning eye:
My fluted bride like a Greek column,
My daughter's face blurred by her breathing,
My diving friends before the war
Shot against waves that seem of marble.

II

I narrow my apertures to see objects in simple contrasts
    of black and white.
I dilate my lenses to light I need to produce an image not
    too faint nor too blurred.
I wear dark-glass filters to shade the boring public glare
    of the self-absorbed midday sun.
I select my angles enlarge my significant details and cut
    my irrelevant impressions from my frame.
I distort the most familiar details to totally new
    hideosities.
Sometimes I watch for hours in a dark square the lamps
    of cars trail ribbons through me.

III

Here are some photographs taken by Venus when she
   rose from the waves:
1) Sprouting breasts of San Marco looked down at from
   the air.
2) *In flagrante* spumings of gods and goddesses in strip-
   tease waters of a fountain in Rome.
3) Curves like whips in air on marble paving stones
   made by chariot wheels at Ephesus.
4) *Vaporetti* setting up the waves that eat away Venetian
   palaces.

Ruin circling ruin circling ruin
And clattering round the toe stubs of antiquity
Tourists spilled from their cars and with their cameras
Clicking clichés of ghosts
Then clambering back and roaring to new graveyards.

The falling bomb photographs the fallen city
The rocket flaming into outer space
Photographs the dwindling Earth before
It lands on a dead star.

A First War Childhood

March 1916,
The middle of a war
– One night long
As all my life –
A child, I lay awake
On my bed under
The slant ceiling
Of the attic of The Bluff,
Our parents' house
On the Norfolk coast.

Beyond the garden
Rain-matted fields
Stretched to the edge
Of the cliff, below which
A roaring Nor'easter
Heaped up waves –
White-maned horses
Charging over rocks

(I thought: 'Deep down under sea
Submarines nose
Among shoals of fish
And waving seaweed
While high above
Zeppelins
Intent to bomb London
Throb through the night.
And near the cliff edge

Soldiers in a dugout
Keep watch on our lives.')

    Wrapped in my blanket
– A chrysalis
Wings not yet sprouted –
I stared up at
The ceiling skylight
Where, mile on mile,
Tons of dark weighed
Pressing on glass,
And stars like jewels
In cogs of a watch
Divided time
Into minutes and seconds.

    Out of that Nowhere
Surrounding all
So that any point anywhere
Was at the centre,
There fell a voice
Like a waterfall
Speaking through space

I AM   I AM   I AM

    Then a bomb exploded –
The night went up
In flame that shook
The shrubbery leaves,
And soldiers came
Out of dark speared with flame,
And carried us children

Into their dugout
Below the earth.

Ear pressed against
The khaki uniform
Of mine, in his arms,
I could hear his heart beat –
With the blood of all England.

Worldsworth

Returned now, seventy years
Later, to the farmhouse
Beside the lake – finding
My way there as by instinct –
A sudden storm shuts down
The enormous view –

                    leaving
Only one drop of rain
Suspended from a leaf –

                    As through
The wrong end of a telescope
I look back to that day
Of August 1916
Our parents brought us here –
Because a Zeppelin,
Turned back from raiding London,
Damaged, across the coast,
Had jettisoned two bombs
Near Sheringham, our home.

                    *

I see in glassy miniature
Each precise particular:

    The van with us all in it
No sooner reaches the farmhouse
By Derwentwater than
We four children scramble out

To climb our first mountain:
CATBELLS its childish name –
With pelt of furze, fern, heather,
As tame for us to mount
As our donkey tethered by
The beach, at Sheringham.

*

Against the skyline, Michael
With arms and legs an X
Yells he has reached the top . . .

*

And all that summer was
Cornucopia that nature
Still pours profuse before me
Within my inmost eye
Like visions the old masters
Made frescoes of on walls:

Us rowing in our boat,
Us fishing, on the lake,
Us walking by the lake
Along the narrow road
A few feet from the water's
Rippling pellucid surface,
Distorting fish and weeds –

And on the road's far side
A ditch, and caves, where ferns
Unfurled heraldic tongues
Of glossy green which, under,
Concealed the dark brown spore.
But more than these I loved
The maidenhair fern with

Stalk fine as the coiled
Hairspring in my watch –
Its leaves minute green spots.

Then, from the road, a path
Led through a wood whose branches
Interweaving above
Seemed high as a cathedral
Sculpting out from shadow
Its own interior, within
Whose hush we stood, and watched
Under our feet the rain,
Dripping from that branched roof,
Collect into small puddles
On which huge black slugs drifted
Like barges on the Thames.

Beyond the wood, we came
Next to a clearing. Then
The rain stopped suddenly: the sky
Seemed one great sword of light
Raised above those bushes
Where berries, red and black,
Blazed like the crown jewels of
Some king much loved in legend
By his peace-loving people
(Among whom none were robbers),
Left on a hedge while he
Went hunting with his followers.

Beyond this there were fields
With slate walls between whose
Rough-hewn slabs, through shadows
Wedged between crevices,

Crystals like pinpoints pricked
Into the dark, their secrets.

But then the path traversed
The naked mountainside
Where, near it, lay the carcass
Of a dead ram, crawled over
By maggots, flies in swarms
As little caring whether
They battened upon eyes
Or guts or blood, as did
Those Zeppelins over London
Whether their bombs destroyed
Temples of stone, or flesh.

*

At dusk,
If there was no rain –

          (great drops
Denting the flattened lake like boulders
Falling in molten lead,
Each one the centre of
Widening concentric circles) –

Our parents,
Seated in deck chairs on the lawn,
Read to each other poems

– The murmuring reached my bed –

Rhythms I knew called Wordsworth
Spreading through mountains, vales,
To fill, I thought, the world.

'*Worldsworth*', I thought, this peace
Of voices intermingling –
'Worldsworth', to me, a vow.

Six Variations

So busy: Pepys at Cambridge, 1660:

February 26: With my father –
Walked in the fields behind King's College
Chapel yard . . . Met Mr Fairbrother
Who took us both to Botolphe's Church
Where Mr Nicholas of Queens preached: text –
  'For thy commandments are broad.'

. . . Thence to dine with Mr Widdrington
Who had with him two fellow commoners
And a Fellow of the college, Mr Pepper . . .
Later, to Magdalen to obtain
The certificate of my brother's entrance –
After which Mr Pechell joined us
And we all sat in the Rose Tavern
Drinking the King's health until dark . . .
Back to our lodging next, then once more
To the Tavern again with Mr Blayton
And Mr Merle with a quart of wine.

I

Such talking drinking life – three hundred
And thirty years ago! Reading, I don't think:
Where are they now, those chatterers? – Thrust
In graveyards? Less than dust – salt sown

In ship-wrecked oceans? Blood-red rust
Of battlefields that crops
Green out of? Left, some relics
Rotting in attics – sword-hilt, snuff box,
Silver or ivory – skeletons
Cased in provincial museums?

II

No, when I read Pepys now, he and his cronies
Burn from their days and through my veins –
Their acts and passions one with those
Moving through mine! As though
To live meant to be tenant of
This temporary flesh through which
Continually the same life flows
Out of the past – through us, and to
Those generations yet unborn.

III

What do I speak but dead men's words?
What are my thoughts but dead men's minds?

IV

Well, there's the being conscious. *Now!*
Each separate life, an 'I' (a world,
To his own self) within which meet
All that's outside: the multitudes
That make this time – and the dead past
Buried within the present – and,
Light-years away, that furthest star

Proved, yet unseen; all pulsing through
My living flesh to make the future.

V

What haunts us now is not those ghosts
From the cased past, but from the future:
Ghosts of the unborn – aviators,
Powered with the means our times invented
To end all life on Earth, and leave
This planet a charred shell within

VI

The elemental Universe
Of minerals, fire, and ice,
Where are
Nor eyes to see nor ears to hear
The planets and the silences
The never-meeting distances
– Nor consciousness, nor Mind, wherein
The shaping atoms recognize
Their world within the words, the names
Met on the tongue, those points of flame.

The Alphabet Tree

(To Valerie Eliot)

Today when I woke
Soon as dawn broke
I saw a ladder
Set up against
The Alphabet Tree.

From on high a Voice spoke
'Today you must climb
Up the rungs of this ladder
Each one a letter
Of words in a poem
That you must write
Rhyme mirroring rhyme,
And complete by midnight
When, from A at the root,
Heaven-reaching, your head
Through the darkness will shoot
To strike letter Z.'

So I climbed up A, B,
C, D, E, F and G,
H, I, J and K
(I was almost halfway!)
And then L, M, N,
O, P, Q, R and S
(Seven more to success!)

U, V and W
(Bets on me double now!)
Until I was up
At the Tree's dizzy top.

So I struck letter Z!
Proud, I then read
The poem in my head.
But 'Alas!' the Voice said:
'Your poem is a flower
Whose petals will scatter
On the breeze in an hour,
Zeroed by Zephyr
And unwept by Zigeuner
Zizzing his zither
Or twanging guitar!

'But behold where on high
The entire ink-black sky
Is diamonded
With stars of great poets
Whose language unfetters
Every Alphabet's letters
Interweaving through Time
In rhythm and rhyme –
Where the living shall read
The more living – the dead!'